DOLPHINS

THE SEA MAMMAL DISCOVERY LIBRARY

Sarah Palmer

Rourke Enterprises, Inc.
Vero Beach, Florida 32964

Library of Congress Cataloging-in-Publication Data

Palmer, Sarah, 1955-
  Dolphins.

  (The Sea mammal discovery library)
  Includes index.
  Summary: Describes, in simple terms, the
appearance, infancy, habits, behavior, and
habitat of the dolphin.
  1. Dolphin—Juvenile literature. [1. Dolphins]
I. Title.
II. Series: Palmer, Sarah, 1955-
Sea mammal discovery library.
QL737.C432P34 1989   599.5'3   88-26430
ISBN 0-86592-363-9

TABLE OF CONTENTS

DOLPHINS

The scientific family name, *Delphinidae*, includes all dolphins and their smaller relatives, porpoises. There are many different kinds of dolphins. One well known kind is the bottlenosed dolphin (*Tursiops truncatus*). It is often seen in films. These dolphins learn tricks very easily. The most common dolphin is *Delphinus delphis*, or common dolphin.

Bottlenosed dolphins are often seen in movies

HOW THEY LOOK

Most dolphins have gray or brown backs with lighter colored undersides. They all look similar. Some have markings that help us to recognize them. Whitesided dolphins have white patches along the sides of their bodies. Killer whales, which are actually large dolphins, have black and white markings. Dolphins grow to an average size of about eight feet. Some kinds can reach twelve feet.

Killer whales are sometimes trained with dolphins

WHERE THEY LIVE

Dolphins live in most of the world's oceans. Common and bottlenosed dolphins can be seen in warm oceans all around the world. They often **breach** or jump close to boats and ships in the Atlantic Ocean. Dolphins also come close to the shore. Some kinds of dolphins, like the Ganges dolphin (*Platanista gangetica*), live in rivers. These dolphins are very different from the ocean livng dolphins.

Dolphins sometimes follow boats into harbor

WHAT THEY EAT

Dolphins eat almost any kind of fish. **Schools** of dolphins and whales sometimes team up to feed on a large group of fish. Common dolphins eat ten to twenty pounds of fish and squid each day. Dolphins are easy to keep in marine parks because their diet is so simple. Their keepers reward them with fish when they do tricks for audiences.

A school of dolphins often means there are fish around

Dolphins love to play in the ocean

Killer whales are very large dolphins

LIVING IN THE OCEAN

Dolphins are very graceful. Their sleek bodies streak through the water and leap through the air. Dolphins' tails are very strong. Steering with their **flippers**, dolphins use their tails to move swiftly through the water. Dolphins are fast swimmers. They can swim at more than 25 M.P.H. over short distances. Like all sea **mammals**, dolphins need to breathe air. They can stay underwater only five minutes, so they do not dive very deep.

Dolphins can swim very fast

THEIR SENSES

Dolphins have very good hearing. They can pick up sounds that people cannot hear. Dolphins use sounds to help them "see" objects underwater. They send whistles and clicks out into the water. When the sounds bounce off objects in the water they make echoes. Every object makes a different echo. Dolphins can tell from the echoes where and what the objects are.

Dolphins can avoid boats by using their excellent sense of hearing

COMMUNICATION

Dolphins talk to each other through a series of clicks, creaks, and whistles. Scientists are still studying the sounds dolphins make. In one experiment, they slowed down a one second dolphin click. They found it was really a series of very fast clicks. Each click that people hear is made up of between 20 and 400 split second clicks. Many people have tried to understand the dolphins' complicated language. So far, nobody has succeeded.

Dolphins communicate with a series of creaks and clicks

BABY DOLPHINS

Female dolphins normally have a single **calf** every two years. The calves are born tail first so they do not drown. A second female dolphin helps the mother to raise her calf to the surface to breathe. At first the calves stay very close to their mothers. As they grow, calves become more curious and swim off alone to play. Still, they return to their mothers' sides as soon as they are called.

Baby dolphins like the safety of their mothers' sides

DOLPHINS AND PEOPLE

People love to watch dolphins perform tricks at the zoo. They leap through hoops and play ball games with their keepers. Dolphins are very intelligent. They learn these tricks quickly and easily. They sometimes add their own ideas for fun! Dolphins will turn almost any object into a game. Young dolphins are especially lively. They are always ready to play.

GLOSSARY

breach (BREECH) — to leap clear of the water

calf (KAV) — a young dolphin

flippers (FLI purz) — winglike limbs that help a dolphin steer through the water

mammals (MAM uls) — animals that give birth to live young and feed them with mother's milk

schools (SKOOLZ) — groups of dolphins

INDEX